The World Is Our Anchor

Emma Wynn

FUTURECYCLE PRESS
www.futurecycle.org

Cover artwork, "Suspension" by Zoë Wilson; cover and interior design by Diane Kistner; ITC Cushing text and Effloresce titling

Library of Congress Control Number: 2023932071

Published by FutureCycle Press
Athens, Georgia, USA

ISBN 978-1-952593-41-3

for my mother, Joan
who is as constant as the Northern Star

Contents

INTERLUDE

Letters Tucked in a Back Drawer

PART II

We Imagine Everything Contained Seeks to Escape

PART I

Watching You Strike Everywhere

Musselled

I'd never eaten them, she said,
mussels, but the stew called for
whole valves flaking black chips.
I know it wasn't the reason
vertigo pinned me flat all night,
  vomiting even water, it was
the movement of the whole world or else
the world was still
  and I was whirling spheres out of tune.
But I felt somewhere
those clots of muscle
folded again in wet darkness
making a home of me—
  inconstant, salty
  dark substrate
on which strange shells
cling and flower.

With a Hymn at the Marrow

My mother sets the bone
as the lamb screams,
drumming with its tiny hooves
in the shackle
of my hands.
The grass under us is gouged to mud
and the lamb's cries steam the air

as my mother wraps the leg,
then holds his whole head in her palm,
murmuring over and over,
soft as wool.
I hunch over his eye, dark
with pain and struggle, trusting

that the hands that hurt
can heal—
that the throat can choose a song,
the broken body rise to fields
on four spindly and perfect legs.

What I Learned from Fairy Tales

It is darkness,
all the stories say,
that is the enemy
and pockmarked faces, still living
after disease, vicious for their scars

to have only the eyes' white in
a face of earth.
To stoop and drag a limb
or lean, wrinkled and worn,
is to hide a cloven hoof.

The oldest lie—
that you can tell a witch
by her Jew's nose
and a saint by her
snow-white skin—

and ones nearly as old—
a virtuous mouth spills
golden coins,
there are iron shoes
to burn the brutal mother,

the beautiful can escape
fathers with wandering hands
and marry princes,
you can live
in glass castles

eating nothing
but golden apples
while the sun glares
everywhere,
hard and white.

Delinquent

The teenagers play redneck
games all summer,

open-door Jeeps and the tinny smack
of baseball bats on mailboxes

all up and down the back roads,
which is where we live,

nothing but back roads
lined with brush and blackbirds.

When Father comes up the hill
with our mailbox, still shoulders

blooming rage,
my sisters dash to bolt holes

or freeze like rabbits and
I'm left

to pass the tools he needs
to beat the box back whole,

sweat itching
like the ache in my gut to burn,

to wind up bursting
with the bile of obedience

and let the black boxes fly
free in the blazing nights.

There are so many ways
to live, but not one of them

is forever.

For the Day the Birds Return

In the muted forests
I practice remembering
the pileated woodpecker, his rowing wings
and shock-red pomp
feeding loud as gunshots on the pines.
Orioles and tanagers, little blades
flashing in the treetops,
the owl-voiced mourning doves
flocking at twilight, which is their color,
and wild turkeys solemn as processions
of nuns through the leaf cover.
Now only my feet scrape the leaves,
breath loud in my ears,
and over and over just
the black-capped chickadee
is calling his own name.

Help Me to Fall

Title and quote "the Lord took the Magdalen's part"
from the writings of St. Teresa of Avila

My grandmother delivered my mother in secret
in the ward of a New York city hospital,
and because the Church said bastard children would be marked,
gave the baby to her sister, who, like the Virgin,
couldn't have a child without grace.
They were all named Mary—
my grandmother, great aunt, and mother
in that good Catholic family.

No surprise, really, that she lives with the nuns now
in Our Lady of Perpetual Sorrow rest home
for bingo and rosaries. They've dug wells
and built schools in Africa, cut umbilical cords
with boiled scissors, shaken scorpions out of morning shoes,
wrapped foot-long worms around sticks and wound them, day by day,
out of their bodies, a bush rosary.
Now they're resting for a moment
before the long reward.

She is sitting somewhere in the rows
at daily Mass, watching grey nuns
arrange the unblessed Host,
their patience broken in as old shoes
sweat-molded to every curve.
The bored priest arrives
to make the magic.
Each white halo sighs and stirs,
creaking to the rail to accept her crumb.

And here she is, my grandmother
in my arms, the rustle of her dry lips at my ear:
The light comes
so strong now
that I'm washed clean of bitterness

and the blood of jungles fills my heart.
Remember, yes—
she grips as if she'll never let me go—
He took the Magdalen's part.
But when I named your mother,
I called her Ellen.

Riding in Iceland

The unrising sun only shadows the sky
as we climb the black rocks,
ponies and riders threading the hills where
the absent light lives instead
low in the moss that glows green in the gaps.

They have their own gait, the ponies
home only on this island. Our guide says it's so soft
a rider can drink a pint without spilling,
but their tolt jolts me down the bones
and I can't find my seat.

There's no way not to be wet—
rain off hood and sleeve almost snow and the air
puffy with fog. At the top, the rock walls disappear
and nothing takes their place.
We dismount creakily for lunch, the ponies

browsing the sparse grass as we gnaw
soggy bread, wondering what it would be like
to ride the world, not as tourists, but saddleless,
easy and shaggy in the drizzle
with a gait wholly our own.

Marveling We Will Reign

Every day I turn over the stone of the world,
ready to be surprised.
I run my fingers through the wet dirt
heavy with the musk of unborn mushrooms.
Its slime is the slick flash of salamander,
who begins life in the swamp and ends
in leaf litter. I too came naked and dripping
from darkness to a skin of fire,
am crouching, muddling through the mud,
knocking against beetles, mycelia, duff—
all our singular lives
rocked in the decaying, astonishing world.

Settled

I know age and children have softened my hips
    and sharpened my tongue.
                I'm sorry
my hunger and my ache are spread so thin
    where once there was only you
and a blaze.
       When the shafts of afternoon
made golden the heat of us
    and every inch of you shone uncommon,
            I hung on your shoulder blades,
    breathing your breath,
temple to temple in the rock of us, and everywhere
    was the strength of spring.

Now I'm drawn as a thread
     rolled between the fingers of midnights,
   nightlight vigils walking children
incandescent with fever   and all their hands and tears
      drinking from my body with their relentless mouths.

   How do I learn to see my right hand?
Bands of tendons in delicate machinery,
     tiny white scar flecks and
puffy branches of blood   chips of nails unevenly cut
so close to me and of me that I'm blind to them.
   Like your gentle endurance
in the endless round
     of laundry, lost hairbands, packed lunches,
     dog shit, guest beds, bus stops
swallowing the bile of patience.

Nothing is as worn as home,
   and I have worn you, too.
Woken you in the early dark, begging for sleep,
   you, stumbling out of our bed,

blurry with exhaustion   to rock babies
      wilting heavy against your shoulder,
    steady in the pale wash of dawn
as ever, holding me.

Tory Hill

Even the locals stopped to admire the twin oaks
on the sloped field, left standing because they were too hard
to shift. When horses and men cleared the field, they built cabins
out of lighter woods and left them, proud Yankees
leaning on no one. The way they stood was
the way they fell.

Did traitor roots lunge for each other out of sight,
tips swollen with unshared sugars, spoiling for touch
and the taste of another? Was it the heat
without shade or the hurricane winds full
across the flat ground or those roots, all lopsided yearning,
that finally brought them down?

The way they wanted to lean, roots and branches, on each other
we denied. In the fever dream of our nation—the strong
finally absolved from all allegiance to the real, the dependence
declared by our bodies inhaling the out-breath of trees,
the fruit of immigrant sweat tart on our tongues.

Yet the split wood knows.
While the mighty stretch proud to the sky
and break brittle on the wind, those of us less singular
tangle underground in the close darkness,
grow reliant, long, and green.

My Father Shows Me Eldraun Lava Field

Somewhere along Iceland's rim road
he stops the car because
I want to see the emptiness.
Wait, wait—only the road is
human, only the poles
and wires edging it!
Beyond, crumbles of black rock bloom
absinthe moss capped
by a low ceiling of fog, grey
like hovering rain.
I can see nothing human
to both horizons.
As always, him showing me
something I can't breathe.

Beneath the wonder is so much
I can't see. What made these fields—
a pressure in the earth like an infection
lanced to clouds of flame and poison
that made the sheep and children lie down
gasping to death.
Air full of drifting grit in the terrible heat,
then a winter that crusted hard
and never seemed to break
freezing the Mississippi as far as New Orleans,
flinging hail to break the cattle's backs.
Even now, the rocks grab and scrape
in their naked fissures.
Only my elbow in his palm lets me lean
on the strength of familiar earth.

It is ten years since I left him,
drew a curtain around my young family,
and threw away the letters that eventually stopped
coming. And is he now
raging into someone else's room

in the pale morning? Are those eyes—
that flared brilliant at old men's stories in bars,
poetry on gravestones, the slow turn
of concert lights over us dancing in the crush—
burning girl children I'll never meet?
It must be grit in my eyes, grit and fog,
when I think of our footprints still out there
on the moss, which takes decades
and decades to heal.

What the Bees Know

I think it must be very ordinary
how the dawn bees nuzzle
the nectaries of the raspberries,
unrolling their soft tongues
and rooting them wearily
in the work of the day.
Again and again, the burrowed sips—
thorax muscles burning,
widening the wings' arcs,
nectar sacs swollen
with boredom and sugar
dragging their way home.

And also ordinary, the days
when it's all sweetness
at the mouths of the flowers
and sweeter still coming home.
The brush of antennae
curving slightly to cup
another's scent, mandibles gentle
on the sides of their faces,
nectar thickening,
as they tremble mouth to mouth.

What the bees know:
distilling honey from each other's
bright, tired mouths
in the ordinary days.

Sleeping Without My Sons

I brought the sheet from home
    but not them—the little one
who pinches my breasts
    with cold fingers and
pushes the blankets off us both
    even as I pull them back
all night long

    and the bigger boy, rolled
in his own blanket with his face
    to the wall,
who kicks me in the darkness
    with untrimmed toenails.
From their parted lips, the slow
    sweet breath of corpses rises.

In this stranger's thin bed
    I keep waking,
arms hanging off to emptiness
    on both sides, while on the floor
the white stripes of dawn
    lie heavy
and bright as steel.
    As if I could hold them,
the light,
    in both hands.

The World Is Our Anchor

We say the glass sweats,
that skim of pebbled drops
so like the weak salt
that shadows our armpits,
necklines, the smalls of our backs.

We imagine everything contained
seeks to escape.
To diffuse, shuck its body,
and rise invisible
above all living
unsullied by dark bread.

Yet the vapor draws down
out of the shocked air, blooming
as it clusters, hydrogen to oxygen,
current to current—
knowing with its body
the way out is in.

We too could come home
to ourselves.
Condense and tremble, newly born
into bonds that lay us skin to skin.

The water comes and goes
like mountains.
If it could speak, it would say we open
and rain from within.

When I Hear Your Broken Voice

for ES

1.

It was just a small paragraph in the local news.
Pocono High found you out, canceled your concert
because you were a lesbian.
I read it over and over. So you were not coming
here, but you were out there
somewhere. Someday, I could find you.

2.

Why, my father said, *are there so many women
at this show?* In your voice, a bird
strong enough to fly south. *I think,*
I said, *they're here together.*

3.

My freshman year I cooked breakfast every Saturday
for two hundred. Chopped onions,
quick-pickled cucumbers, and wrestled dough
into and out of the kneading machine, its bowl
tall as my thigh. Always your voice
in the background, golden
and rich as oil, alive
with the yeasty smell of bread rising
and rising.

4.

Yesterday, I heard a woman on the radio
imitating you poorly, each note a wavering ghost
circling without alighting.
It was you.

5.

And you won't talk about it, the secret
in plain view. Like your mullet, your plaid,
your slight wife. I have no right to ask,
but I need your truth again.
Tell me, like you did before, that it will be fine

to grow old—
for our heads to wobble, short-circuited,
our nerves betraying us—to weaken,
brown, and sag. I can believe it
if you tell me once more
it is fine:

her lips against my hair, this body
that only knows how to keep going
in your echo.

Memorial to Steller's Sea Cow

The calves snort and whuffle in the canopy kelp,
    ten-ton fathers hovering like storm clouds
        or a shoal of islands, grey and pitted.
Above them gulls, men flying
    in bone-smooth boats
        whose hooks, ozone bright,
burn and catch. Then the drag
    and crush of air, peeled skin
        and almond-sweet fat in soft smears.
Scratching a hunt on their bones—the spear,
    the spray and thrash, round bodies
        floating like moons. Carve it here—
everything that rises we harpoon.

There Are No Words for What We Do

At Perkins School for the Blind
teachers slapped with rulers
the girl rocking gently with a secret smile,
one heel tucked up
under her skirts.

There's always someone
ready to spoil a girl's fun—
sad Jesus with a lamb,
Sylvester Graham and his bread of abstention
crumbling to dust on the tongue.

So we learn to grow so small.
Under a blanket in the back seat,
sunlight a wash through closed lids,
trickles of knee-pit sweat
sticking to leather,
the last puzzle piece
slotted in at last.

All the strays
are coming home. God's city coming
slowly out of the clouds
like a silver ship.
The day's film rewinding.
A cup shattering itself whole.

Just a girl's body
humming
a brighter chord
down the bones.

Host

A fire in the wind
blousing smoke, then molten
pebbles I can hardly go near to stir.
Everything outside its circle
brightens as it fades—
cattle fences, briar,
the salt of stars.
Horizon a pale line
reflecting distant cities.

No one comes.
The beers I don't drink
shine with sweat. Circled benches
warm their invisible bones.
Oak feathers to ash,
what was solid walks on air.
Then the firefly lights of phones
and you stumbling, laughing,
across the grass.

Things We Lost to the Flood

Alternate uses for pencils,
their flat shafts reeling in the tissue-thin
black tentacles of mix tapes.
The mix tape. Frilled notebook-paper messages
passed forward in Health class
"i's" dotted with hearts like
slips of light in our pockets, washed
to pulp in our jeans. Little white pebbles
we could hold in our palms.

Consulting oracles—older brothers
who knew the first names of drummers
and where to buy that beer
that tasted of rye, the smart route
to Philadelphia. Rarely knowing where we were
or how long it would take to get there,
maps like sails flapping dangerously.
How easy it was to wash up on strange shores,
to wander into strange bars,
into local disputes over the way home.

On the Meditation that Exchanges Self & Other

after Santideva

While we're still mistaken
about the nature of things,
let me hold you on my lap, you
cage of bones veiled in flesh,
our tongues arasp and tangled.
Not in my bliss alone
until that final moment,
when the plain of light opens
and clenches like a fist.
I see for a moment everything
on which we depend: no eternity,
merely the body's beloved filth.
Clot of earth, fellow traveler,
mouth raining blossoms.

Three Hours from Morning

Little Finn startles upright from sleep
and, wide-eyed, vomits across our bed
the celery and noodle soup
I cooked when he was hungry,
a thin and sour broth.
I half wake
and, more from instinct than thought,
flip him—one hand cupping his whole forehead,
the other thumb under his armpit
and palm against his rib cage—
as he heaves and chokes,
cries thick with spittle and shock.
A last shudder wrings him
and, just as quickly, he falls back on the pillow
and into sleep—this child
who will outgrow my hand, shiver
and retch someday on cold tile
in a strange home.
I'm wiping the flush sweat from his eyelids
with my shirt, praying—
May I haunt you in your
pain as you ripped me to arrive here
in this world where the body breaks
and swells and breaks again.
When I am broken
beyond all sickness and you,
may you be brushed by the ghost
of my hands, which can live
if you do.

On C Block

Meagan and Sophi are transgender women incarcerated in a men's facility in California. While state regulations permit them to request to be transferred to a women's prison, they fear that doing so would separate them and have elected to remain where they are.

In the men's prison, San Diego,
Meagan and Sophi tell me they love
to feed the sparrows and the brown
rabbits that huddle
low in the grass.

If they sit so still
their own bodies forget them,
a rabbit brushes by like a sigh.

Sometimes Sophie runs and runs
miles round the track in her
taped-up shoes, watching the birds
skip the fence
and dart for the mountains.

At night, they open their tray slots
and reach out their arms.
Their fingers, dark with dirt,
can just touch.

The Meadow

It was the one place my father never mowed
    when he was driven to cut
whatever he could reach—
    that slow dip and broad basin of earth.
So it grew tangled with wild roses, sharp
    grasses, cornflower and snakes,
little furred animals rustling in the weeds,
    also whatever stalked them,
and grasshoppers thick as thumbs
    whirring a drone of invisible wings.
On summer nights, the air was flecked
    with sparks that settled and paired,
mated, rose again.
    Our mother, who knew a cage,
would not let us jar and keep them.

In the spring, icy water poured off the hills
    and turned it all to marsh, a loamy sponge
eager to swallow small feet and goldfinches
    that dropped to the swaybacked
tips of seeding grasses like coins
    flipped from the sky.
Barely grown ourselves,
    I bring you home to see
the lightning bugs open the night
    under the weak mirror of stars.
I point but cannot say *Look!*
    This is my childhood
field!—poppies fat with heat,
    the starred sky so close,
close, too, the thorns
    and their embrace of blood,
the curved teeth of the rattler
    and the warning of its tail.

Kernel

Inspired by Peter Wohlleben

After the drought,
our beech trees break into prodigal blossom,
desperate for posterity and
faithless to the rain.
It is the battered
that burst most in bloom.

Recklessly, sap swells the spindle buds
and the leaves unfold naked
of the usual defenses,
no power left to poison.
The beech leaf miners bite once
and, full of sweetness, ravage.

By fall, burrs peel back
from the gloss of nuts drying and
cracking open in the shade.
But a nail splitting each triangular shell
reveals nothing—the heart of this
wild effort, empty.

To be emptied is to be full.
To be battered without bitterness
is to bloom spacious
at one's heart
and nourish, unknowing,
the lives of others.

Closer

Every room
   is a place I'm waiting
      for you to arrive.

Then you're not yet beside me,
   not yet with your hands
      on my neck.

When, like geese flying south,
   we're locked together
      in solitary flight,

I catch on your face
   the moment you go
      farthest from me,

grip my shoulders
   shining with surprise
      that you're so good

there, deep inside,
   where I send you
      and cannot go.

Homecoming

All through France, and later Germany, when his unit
settled for the night in copses, barns, town houses
with bombed-off faces, tents in mud, my grandfather
readied himself to survive as for prayer.
First he'd find a piano, buy time with an egg,
then wash his socks and hang them to dry
before morning. All around him, foot rot
and privates drinking kerosene,
swaying to their own shattered music.

So he came home unbroken, contraband Nazi
banner ripped from a pole smuggled home in spare trousers.
Married glamorous *goyim* women,
tucked a baby grand under a velvet quilt
at night, bought a silver *keter* for the synagogue,
furs and theatre tickets, pickled tomatoes
and sandwiches fisted full of brisket,
demanded burnt toast in diners,
kept a beautiful beard
and four children, a Cadillac.

Remember, my dad laughs,
when he came home
to leave groceries at the door, you could just
wave goodbye to him going down the stairwell
if you ran? My aunt puts her hand over his.
In her house, last year's Christmas tree still hangs with glass
glitter and brittle brown arms,
one slip from going up in flames.

It's 1996, Clinton launches cruise missiles on Iraq,
grandfather bleeds out
in Beth Israel, it's late, and Dad's car
tears out, the red wash of headlights
on my bedroom wall shrinking into the night.

We sleep easy as soldiers,
until it's almost a relief to hear the bombs
begin to whistle their way home.

At the Lake

June 19, 2020

The preschoolers patter wet footprints
across the deck, chattering
in their fading lisps,
loom delighted over fishes, squeal.
A brown rat paddles the shallows,
imagined teeth sharp
as thrills.

What's not here is not.
Rioting police with their acids,
viruses that drown grandparents on dry land
like the coastal cities scrambling
their breakwaters.

The trees' dark skirts
creep down the sand.
In the shade, parents ready to run
for the small head going under,
legs churning like a prayer

that small legs find
a lake bed ramped to air.
Which surrounds us,
yes—
even the faithless,
even rats.

Ebb Tide

The sea's glimmer has gone down
        and I walk out on new ground
streaked with bile-colored foam
                and tangles of wet weed, the reek
of the crotch of the sea.
                At my foot,
        a half-eaten fish, silver-skinned
head and tail bridged by a ladder of bone.
        A crab scuttles sideways,
waving his clippers.
                The gulls scream and dive
        and, briefly,
                he flies.
They empty him in swarms.

Some days it's like this—
        the mercy of men   a flurry of beaks,
        squatting in the sand,
                nauseous with exhaustion
and spent grace, trying
        to open my sharp arms
to the emptiness,
                which is all
        we can ever hold.

Beasts

Alone in the steer barn, my mother
forgets the rules. Squeezing between bull
and board wall, she is pinned,
and neither wood nor hide will give
so she must.
The lights buzz like bluebottle flies,
spring cage ribs press her rabbit heart,
and I, tadpole in the darkness,
quiver in the blueshift of her blood.

Yet we didn't end there, before my beginning.
Your mercy, if that's what it was,
rolled you slow to lean instead on open air.
We hung on a horn, my mother and I,
in the heave of oxygen's flush,
gasping in the grace of your roughage.

Now, in the potluck days of summer,
I balance my plates of vegetables,
my flickering gaze that skips the plates
slick with pinked fat, other people's children
little birds gaping for the animals they know how to name
but not that they devour. Only I see
we feast with ghosts.

But when sorrow rises in my throat
like floodwater and friends' faces loom
vicious and strange, I feel you
breathe my breath,
your hooves soft on my shoulders,
the embrace of one child for another
on the killing room floor.

When You Ask the Night for Answers

The trees lie down
on the snow
like tattoos on an arm,
their upright shadows
gone
against the sky.

On the porch, in the wind,
no longer grasping
the rail, you open
your hands.
The moon's pale fire
whitens in each palm.

River Walking

Snapweed favors the wet
    banks of the melt stream, cutting ripe
through the forest's darker ferns
    and brambles, a bright pod
curious legs can split along the seam
    of glimpsed water.
Spotted orange flowers dangle
    from threads, bobbing
for bees. Water so clear it lies.
    The pebbles sparkled with quartz
and grass blowing in the current
    aren't pressed under glass;
it's deeper than ankles, cold
    as nothing living,
the only rushing and speaking thing
    among the trees walking
slow as ages. I push upstream,
    skirting muds pits in silted pools,
waterfalls and stretches of rocky rills
    tiered like canal locks, overgrown
and boatless. Each step through green
    serene and blind as branches
and the indifferent water's
    glimmer and chatter, ceaseless
refusing, as I lean down,
    to reflect my face.

A Perfect Mother

Last night the boys fought in their sleep,
whining each other's names and kicking
until I rolled the baby off to slot myself
between them, burning.
All day long my eyelids creak.
The little one is hollow-leg hungry
and begs for the swing
until my elbows ache, this poem
swelling like an abscess in my throat.

Lunch, a vegetable, screaming.
Finn toddles into the bathroom just
to check where I am—here!
Where else?
They must see it, my brittle smolder
brush rough through their tangles.
How I want to swim out
past the buoys
and just keep going.

Instead, I lift Finn into the bucket swing
and set it going
back and forth, apologizing
in silent rhythm. Pushing him away
over and over, as
regular as rain,
he rocks back, laughing,
into my arms.

After All Our Years

I know some day I'll wake up alone
or you will.
The dawn will draw us out of sleep
and, in those first moments, we'll forget,
throw out our arms, grasping half-asleep
like babies who startle closed
when you let go.

We'll wrap around nothingness
and then come cold awake,
hands on the rough linen of the sheet,
the water of grief rising in our throats.
I can write it, but we won't—
only you or only I
will ever wake alone.

INTERLUDE

Letters Tucked in a Back Drawer

The intent [of my writing] …is not to *give voice* to [those erased by history], but rather to imagine what cannot be verified, a realm of experience which is situated between two zones of death—social and corporeal death—and to reckon with the precarious lives which are visible only in the moment of their disappearance.… It is a history of an unrecoverable past; it is a narrative of what might have been or could have been; it is a history written with and against the archive.

—Saidiya Hartman, "Venus in Two Acts"

In the Nature of Things

In 1857, the famed abolitionist Charles Sumner sailed for Europe to recover from the brutal beating he received on the Senate floor at the hand of Preston Brooks. He left behind his dear friend, Samuel Gridley Howe, founder of the Perkins School for the Blind, fellow abolitionist, and crusader for prison and school reform. Despite Samuel's dedication to multiple progressive causes, he expected his wife, Julia Ward Howe, to be a housewife and opposed her career as an author and public intellectual. She would later surpass him in fame by writing "The Battle Hymn of the Republic."

Phrases from the title and lines 8-11, 23-25, 29-30, 37, 40, 50-55, 57-58, 63, 70-71, and 73-75 are taken from the letters, papers, and published works of Charles Sumner, Samuel Gridley Howe, and Julia Ward Howe.

1. Letter from Charles Sumner to Samuel Gridley Howe (unsent)
    Shipboard en route to Paris, 1857

I will never send this letter
because I know your feelings,
the spasming sea flashes light
in telegraphic stutters that batter my words
back at me, a Morse code spelling "traitor."
There has been between us an
unspoken agreement to lie
but the inborn, invincible sentiments
of my human heart, nature
in all her subtle forces
is marshalled against us
and I am not strong enough not
to wish you loved me with your body
as well as your mind.
My broken head still bears
the mark of Brooks' cane
and I wish you were here to gentle it,
beside me in my narrow bed
when I wake thrashing,
again ripping the desk from the floor to defend myself
and escape. All my life
I've burned to break others' chains,
sunder the hateful embrace of Slavery,
but my own depraved longing for you
I cannot subdue.

I have said, Love, that no man
should own another, but
I would be yours
until the sun and moon and stars
have all passed away.

2.   Letter from Samuel Gridley Howe to Charles Sumner (unsent)
     Boston, 1858

Perhaps it is my work among the blind—
learning to see with the tips of my fingers,
listening for voices to tremble and fall
or crack bitter with anger, to know others
when all the faces around me are closed—
but I see more than you know.
We live in inhuman systems, prisons and asylums
where those so disposed find only madness,
the plantation and auction block
rotten timbers in the foundation of our nation.
Even our village schools,
where pupils are cuffed and thrashed
for stupidity and brilliance alike.
In the midst of all this,
what does our happiness mean,
thee and me?
You know me, dear Charles,
a man much given to dark moods
in need of constant care
and care for others is a woman's nature.
So Julia is my love
as a wife. Yet I cannot help signing,
as I never can help, that I am
and forever shall be
entirely yours.

3.   Letter from Julia Ward Howe to Samuel Gridley Howe (unsent)
     Boston, 1857

I never told you, but I heard you and Charles
laughing at unmarried women
and their barren lives
as if you knew what we wanted
to create. I have born
one book only, and that a dangerous labor
that near killed our marriage.
What we saved, a buried kind of life.
Scribbling poems on scraps I hide in drawers
tugged at by the book in my pocket
as I write the grocer,
dandle a baby, serve all and dinner,
set my teeth, and brightly
draw you from your regular darkness.
I wrote Annie, "I am trying
to press all bitterness out of my heart,"
but I lied. Samuel,
mark no steadfast path for me, I am
and will myself a comet
dire and strange.

Comfort From Abroad

Joshua Fry Speed and the young lawyer Abraham Lincoln shared rooms and a bed above Speed's store from 1837 to 1841 in Springfield, Illinois. In 1840, Speed's father died, and Joshua began making plans to return to Kentucky to take charge of the family's plantation, Farmington. As the date of Speed's departure approached, Lincoln broke off his engagement to Mary Todd and fell into a deep depression. Joshua wrote that Lincoln "went crazy. [I] had to remove razors from his room—take away all knives and other such dangerous things. It was terrible." When Joshua left, Lincoln wrote to his law partner: "Whether I shall ever be better I can not tell: I awfully forebode I shall not. To remain as I am is impossible; I must die or be better, it appears to me." Within a year, both Lincoln and Speed were married to women.

Lines 1, 5, 6, 10, & 18 contain excerpts from letters Lincoln wrote to Speed just after their marriages.

To Abe, January 1841 (found among Speed's papers after his death)

Love, very shortly you will again feel well.
You and I were strangers once, so might her
face grow sweet. Know the heart can fall again that fell.

Our ends are wives, the normal hearth. You can tell
the bargain bad? Hug it all the tighter,
love. Very shortly you will again feel well.

Now forget our little rooms. Our bed we'll sell
and put away with childish things, lighter
leave, as men from boys to duty hereto fell.

For there's nothing but what earth can realize—hell
nor heaven—toilless fields nor bach'lor nights for
ever bright, but youthful dreams that die as well

in Kentucky dust as anywhere I'd dwell.
The frontier ends, dear. All have their plight or
yoke no day will lift, God-given. Our house fell.

Forget the steamboat to St. Louis (don't tell),
our slender bunk, let mem'ry grow slighter
love—very shortly you will again feel well.
Green hearts fade, must age and turn, in falling, fell.

Love Is the Watchword

Bayard Rustin was a peace, civil rights, and gay rights activist. His influence led Martin Luther King Jr. to embrace the nonviolent tactics for which the latter is famous. Despite being shunned by King for years after a U.S. Representative threatened to tell the media that King and Rustin were lovers as well as public attacks by Senator Strom Thurmond, who called Rustin a "sex pervert" on the Senate floor, Rustin never denied being gay. Rustin's lover, Davis Platt, said, "If anybody asked him, he would have told the truth."

Lines 4 and 5 contain lines from the song, "Goin' Home Boys," by Josh White and the Carolinians, with whom Rustin performed in the 1940s. During World War II, Rustin sang "A Stranger in a Distant Land" to German POWs being transported on a train though Texas. Lines 18, 19, 23, and 24 contain quotes by Rustin from public speeches and writings. The title of the poem comes from a song that Rustin wrote for the Montgomery Improvement Association in 1955 or 1956.

From the journal of Davis Platt, found after his death on October 3, 2008

Not waiting like the rest of us
for the light to change. You
were the tenor on the train

singing   *time is up, boys,*
throw those chains away.
          Every German POW
just another white boy

hanging on your voice.
No one knew how to be your enemy,
     sweet fool

integrating even your Kentucky prison
until they locked you alone
in a room where the white lights
          never burned out.

Who did you hold there, forehead
a dark moon, whiskey voice
in his ear?

Even the stones, you said,
would cry out if you did not.
I wanted only your electric mouth

and you, the streets
and buses where they beat you.
When you said   we must tuck our bodies places

so the wheels don't turn, you meant
not in my arms.
But I've never been sorry.

Watching you strike everywhere
    like lightning,
guileless, elemental,

impossible to resist.

PART II

We Imagine Everything Contained Seeks to Escape

Lifting

First, we practice standing on the ground,
not as if we need permission or
perched on our toes like Barbies,
but as if we grew out of it.

We shoulder the bar, shift our feet,
assume the day's iron weight.
Knees torqued outward just slightly,
our thighs shiver and grip.

Stippled with the itch of sweat we can't let go to scratch,
we squat, then surge to standing, mothers
refusing to disappear into our babies' mouths
or shrink, pretty and pleasant,

bearing it. True here
what isn't in life:
What doesn't kill you
makes you stronger.

American Sutra

In a pool at the cliff's edge   Finn bathes, royal
with the upright back   of the newly sitting,
slaps his hands, startles splashes   into his eyes, laughing,
then does it again.

Off the drop, hardwood forest   spreads across three states
like a rumpled green cloth   the spilled water of lakes in every dip
and crumbs of rocks left scattered   by glaciers that moved
across Connecticut like cattle cars.

Asher climbs the waterfall to higher pools   and lies flat on his naked belly
to float leaves, bark, clots of mud   down the stream, crying
Finn, Finn, look—catch them!   The baby squeals, flails, and
goes under.

Doron pulls him grinning from the pool   wraps him in a shirt
and my arms. His hair under my chin   smells cleanly of dirt
while only feet from us   the water vanishes
and the air begins.

Why I Daily Wear Black

Because it is the color of ravens
who haunt poets and stalk boldly.

In its silence the eye can rest.
Because, at night, the sky disappears

and a veil lifts on a thousand suns.
To wear my shadow honestly.

Because it contains the rainbow in secret
and preserves my nectar from bees.

To bury my hands in the sun-warmed fur
of endings.

Why I daily wear black
skin and cloth, paper and words.

Gifts

What you own, my father said
    owns you, you have to practice
giving it away. In middle school
    he biked a paper route for months
to fill a tank with fish—neons,
    zebras, fish with glass skin
whose stomachs glowed rose
    at the heart of their outlines.
Given to a friend whose uneasy parents
    tried to reject the outsized
gesture, but he made it a habit never
    to look back. After Grandpa died,
his favorite coat the faux chinchilla
    with the chemical-green lining
still smelling of pipes in which
    I slouched across college quads
until it fell to shreds. His first car
    the Black Beetle, undrivable with its
British wheel, his best friend Maurey,
    who stepped off into air
while hiking, its invisible passenger.
    Guitars left behind changing
countries, hundred-dollar bills to waitresses,
    a puppy. He gave until he was so light
he could walk away from anything.
    The last time I saw him—
his pocket stuffed with plane tickets,
    breathing the steam of his coffee
and making promises, the gleam
    of his eye and half-body hug,
then his coat disappearing
    in the snow—a trip I never let him
come home from. His daughter, first
    to the punch, learned from the best:
You cannot lose
    the things you give away.

Sisters

For KMS

When we climbed the forest hills to the tree
    etched with bark beetle trails we thought
        were the hieroglyphs of fairies,

stepped between the side jambs
    of upright saplings, aching to arrive
        in Narnia, where the good are saved,

when we bound each other with double-dutch rope
    and strained in the panic and delight
        of being held as we struggled,

when we cupped the lightning bugs soft
    in our palms, hollowed out the forsythia
        to play fortress under its yellow crown,

when we fought with knives,
    kissed boys in the basement, cooked each other
        midnight omelets, sang dirty songs

behind closed doors,
    when we swung through the night air
        filthy with woods mud and high

above the house lights, you and me—
    that was when we ran
        wild and good.

What We Add

It is not the stones
that nestle close as lovers

or shiver
under a skin of ice

but the ghost of my mind
that builds from them a wall.

The stones themselves
lie on one another
like stones.

And me—
the darting speed

with which I harden,
melt, and am transformed

like a mountain strange,
no sooner born
than gone.

Planet B

We're taking only what we use:
the cows we've bred placid, gargantuan,
our good workers, pine and bamboo,
the woods that grow fast and straight,
and cartons of strawberries, swollen polyploidy.

We've stripped the beds, both flower and sea,
and emptied every larder back to bones,
left the woolly-stalked begonia
that wandered in the hardwood shade,
the bluebuck—useless, beautiful,
its ringed horns as long as an arm.

As a packing song, let's name the dead:
Mount Glorious day frog,
the Xerces blue,
Xysmalobium baurii.
The Ascension crake
that could not fly.

In the room that was the living,
melancholy touches us
like the shadow of a bird. Now
only slabs of sunlight suspend the dust.
On the stoop, we join the meats and oils
barrelled, boxed, and bound
for no other home.

Conjunctions

Last night Jupiter and Saturn drew so close
they became one light.

Above our balcony,
only a ceiling of clouds.

So that was once in a lifetime,
the hidden miracle,
only once.

First breath
unfolding my son like a poppy.

Looking up from salting the path as
new snow lights on trees.

Weighing this book in a dry palm
before you open it.

It's all only once,
always becoming one light.

Acknowledgments

Grateful acknowledgment goes to the following publications in which these poems first appeared, some in earlier versions:

805: "When I Hear Your Broken Voice"
Apricity Press: "Lifting"
Delmarva Review: "Help Me to Fall"
Fatal Flaw Literary Magazine: "What the Bees Know"
peculiar: "In the Nature of Things"
Poetry South: "Things We Lost to the Flood," "There Are No Words for
 What We Do"
Prime Number Magazine: "Moving Day"
Raw Art Review: "Tory Hill," "Kernel," "Marveling We Will Reign"
Sky Island Journal: "The Meadow," "Settled"
Subnivean Magazine: "Homecoming," "Gifts," "Ebb Tide," "Riding in Iceland,"
 "Memorial to Steller's Sea Cow," "A Perfect Mother"
SWIMM Every Day: "Sleeping Without My Sons"
Waxing & Waning Journal: "My Father Shows Me Eldraun Lava Field"
West Trade Review: "The World Is Our Anchor"

"Beasts" appeared in the anthology *Passionate Penholders II* (Wingless Dreamer, 2019).

The following poems appeared in *Help Me to Fall,* Moonstone Arts Center 2019 chapbook prize winner (Moonstone Press, 2020): "My Father Shows Me Eldraun Lava Field," "Three Hours from Morning," "Moving Day," "What I Learned from Fairy Tales," "Tory Hill," "Settled," "The Meadow," "Marveling We Will Reign," "Sisters," "Why I Daily Wear Black," "Kernel," "In the Nature of Things," "After All Our Years," "Help Me to Fall," "Lifting," "Beasts," "The World Is Our Anchor."

About FutureCycle Press

FutureCycle Press is dedicated to publishing lasting English-language poetry in both print-on-demand and Kindle formats. Founded in 2007 by long-time independent editor/publishers and partners Diane Kistner and Robert S. King, the press was incorporated as a nonprofit in 2012. A number of our editors are distinguished poets and writers in their own right, and we have been actively involved in the small press movement going back to the early seventies.

Each year, we award the FutureCycle Poetry Book Prize and honorarium for the best original full-length volume of poetry we published that year. Introduced in 2013, proceeds from our Good Works projects are donated to charity. Our Selected Poems series highlights contemporary poets with a substantial body of work to their credit; with this series we strive to resurrect work that has had limited distribution and is now out of print.

We are dedicated to giving all of the authors we publish the care their work deserves, offering a catalog of the most diverse and distinguished work possible, and paying forward any earnings to fund more great books. All of our books are kept "alive" and available unless and until an author requests a title be taken out of print.

We've learned a few things about independent publishing over the years. We've also evolved a unique and resilient publishing model that allows us to focus mainly on vetting and preserving for posterity poetry collections of exceptional quality without becoming overwhelmed with bookkeeping and mailing, fundraising activities, or taxing editorial and production "bubbles." To find out more, come see us at futurecycle.org.

The FutureCycle Poetry Book Prize

All original, full-length poetry books published by FutureCycle Press in a given calendar year are considered for the annual FutureCycle Poetry Book Prize. This allows us to consider each submission on its own merits, outside of the context of a traditional contest. Too, the judges see the finished book, which will have benefitted from the beautiful book design and strong editorial gloss we are famous for.

The book ranked the best in judging is announced as the prize-winner in January of the subsequent year. There is no fixed monetary award; instead, the winning poet receives an honorarium of 20% of the total net royalties from all poetry books and chapbooks the press sold online in the year the winning book was published. The winner is also accorded the honor of being on the panel of judges for the next years competition; all judges receive copies of the contending books to keep for their personal library.

Printed in the USA
CPSIA information can be obtained
at www.ICGtesting.com
LVHW021958300823
756751LV00003B/304